Edited by Robert Wallace
With drawings by Neal Crosbie

Bits Press
Cleveland

The acknowledgments on page 146 constitute a continuation of this copyright notice. To all the poets the editor says loudly, Many thanks. Readers who wish also to say thanks for this poem or that are encouraged to write to the poets c/o Bits Press. Poets are people, as James Wright once said, so say hello.

Light Year '84 is partially supported by a grant from the Ohio Arts Council.

Printed and bound in the U.S.A. by Walsworth Publishing Company, Marceline, Missouri.

ISBN: 0-933248-02-4

Light Year, the annual of new light verse and funny poems, welcomes submissions. Recent previously published poems are OK. SASE, please. To:

> Bits Press
> Department of English
> Case Western Reserve University
> Cleveland, Ohio 44106

Jog on, jog on, the footpath way,
And merrily hent the stile-a;
A merry heart goes all the day,
Your sad tires in a mile-a.

CONTENTS

1

WHAT KIND OF GUY WAS HE?

Just so you shouldn't have to ask again,
He was the kind of guy that if he said
Something and you were the kind of guy that said
You can say that again, he'd say it again.

Howard Nemerov

PILLOWS

I love the ladies with cats on their laps,
The langorous ladies with cats on their laps,
Who seem to be listening twice to what you say,
And fondling, fondling, would never get up and walk away.

Not even if Pavarotti were singing.
Not even if the telephone were ringing.
Not even if you were rude, or cried.
Not even if the cat died.

Bonnie Jacobson

THE CLARINET IS A DIFFICULT INSTRUMENT

I was eating minestrone when I heard something fall
outside my apartment window.
It was too dark to see anything
but a pair of arms slam shut a window
on the third floor of the building opposite mine.

In the morning, all I could find in the yard
was a bent clarinet.
Its horn was dented, a key was missing,
the pawn shop sticker still said nine dollars.

It reminded me of the French explorer,
Antoine de la Mothe Cadillac.
He too had dreams, set sail up the St. Lawrence
looking for China,
and wound up settling in Detroit instead.

Michael Finley

MONROEVILLE, PA.

One day a kid yelled
"Hey Asshole!"
and everybody on the street
turned around

Ed Ochester

THE GODFATHER'S NURSERY RHYME

This little piggy went to Florence;
This little piggy went to Rome.
This little piggy went to Palermo,
And this little piggy stayed home,
But THIS little piggy
Played it smart. See.
He stuck this macaroni in his cap
And went to Fort Lee, New Jersey
Where he shot everybody up
And made a lotta money.

James Camp

BRATS

At the market Philbert Spicer
Peered into the cold-cut slicer —
Whiz! the wicked slicer sped
Back and forth across his head,
Quickly shaving — what a shock! —
Fifty chips off Phil's old block,
Stopping just above the eyebrows.
Phil's not one of them there highbrows.

Doris Drummond sneaked a look
In a locked and cobwebbed book,
Found some secret words you said
That could summon up the dead.
Sad to say, the dead she summoned
Had it in for Doris Drummond.

A hiss! A gulp! — Where are you, Niles?
Why is your huge pet snake all smiles?
Are you in there, you little dickens,
Where it kind of lumps and thickens?

Greg has trained a pig that grunts
Greek and Latin, both at once.
What is more, it plays Monopoly,
But, I must say, rather sloppily.

Thinking it hard candy, Rube
Gobbled down a Rubik's cube.
His stomach, in one revolution,
Came up with the right solution.

Noticing an open-doored
Spacecraft, Nora sneaked aboard.
Now where is she?
                      Moved, poor dear,
Several million miles from here.

Camping in Grand Canyon Park,
Bertram, as the sky grew dark,
And the first star climbed the sky,
Told a grizzly nine feet high,
"Beat it, b'ar! Don't hang around!
Find your own darned camping ground!"

Sunset grieved, and evening star,
When poor Bertram crossed the b'ar.

Dora Dutz, that little stinker,
Skinny-dipped in fabric shrinker.
We will find her yet, we hope,
Once we buy a microscope.

Vince released a jar of vermin
During Mister Drowser's sermon
On how cheerfulness is catching.
Soon the whole next pew was scratching.

John, while swimming in the ocean,
Rubbed sharks' backs with suntan lotion.
Now those sharks have skin of bronze
In their bellies — namely, John's.

Stealing eggs, Fritz ran afoul
Of an angry great horned owl.
Now she has him — what a catch! —
Seeing if his head will hatch.

X. J. Kennedy

ON BEING MUCH BETTER THAN MOST AND YET NOT QUITE GOOD ENOUGH

There was a great swimmer name Jack
Who swam ten miles out — and nine back.

John Ciardi

AERIAL

". . .I feel profoundly sad when they collaborate in sorrow drenched cantatas by Keiser or Allessandro Scarlatti. I am lifted up to the dramatic heights they scale in Handelian operatic arias. I suspect I could almost achieve levitation above an uncomfortable seat when they close with a humorous aria by Baldassare Galuppi. Need I say more?. . ."

review of Philidor Trio,
Rochester Democrat and
Chronicle

We barely noticed him, starting to play,
the little man in the stiff toupee,
shaking his program, biting his pen,
shifting about in his seat — but then

All of a sudden, by God! He flew!
Over and under, around and through,
skylight and curtain, spot and strut,
missing the chandelier by a foot!

"Play! Keep playing!" I had to shout
above the roar as the crowd rushed out,
except for a scattering, here and there,
of those who flung back their heads to stare.

"Play! Keep playing!" One final note:
he drifted, hovered, began to float
back toward his seat. I whispered to Sue,
"I think we can count on a good review. . ."

Bruce Bennett

WILL YOU FORGIVE ME FOR SAYING

Grand opera is overrated
Is overstuffed, is overstated

Is overloud, is overlong —
In short an overdose of song?

Just too too too too too much clover.
The Peace of God when it's all over.

Robert Francis

TAMBOURINE

You think of gypsies, kindergarten brats,
and the glassy-eyed bimbo, always the least
adept of the group that calls itself musicians.
What does she do but bang it on her butt?

Pop and hiss, those contrarieties,
caught as they are in the tambourine's eternal
hoop, squabble, their bass and treble demands
upon our flagging attention, stupid, vulgar.

And music condescends to this, or aspires:
Baron Ochs, however else he is gross,
recoups a little, doesn't he, of our hearts,
baring his own with that simple wistful waltz,

its shallow depths his right and limpid pool?
What we remember of all the refinement, nuance,

and complication simplifies to that,
and the tambourine is the virtuoso player

of simplification flirting with boredom. Guess
if she or it be instrument for the other
to play — for we are not so circumscribed
as she. Acknowledge the little frisson they make

together, elemental, accomodating,
even promiscuous (any tune will do),
or close your eyes as hers are closed and conjure
any face you will. Dumb as she is,

she knows how it is, how she's put upon,
but doesn't seem to mind as she dishes out
lucidities prefabricated for these
healthy inarticulate creatures, the forms

of feeling, the right vessels for that wine
their lives' cuvée may provide. The best will age,
mellow, deepen, but keep that scintillant
character, the nerves' tambourine thrill,

abstract, impersonal, and yet expressive
of what they are. Fortune, good or ill,
will compose the score, filling out the staves —
which is why gypsies, children in rhythm bands,

and adolescents, careering into the future,
like so well what most of us just suffer.
They bang and jangle, playing, thoughtless, eager,
happy, blindly happy. That's the skill.

David R. Slavitt

HERE I AM

Here I am standing
at the toilet bowl
overlooking a cemetery
and, as I look down
at my own foregone conclusion,
calmly piss.

David Ignatow

NOT HAVING WINGS

If I had a wing it might hurt,
be broken. I would trail it
around, stumbling on it. Maybe infection
sets in. Tortured by terrible pain
I forget all about God and curse
and am lost. I'm glad I don't have any wings.

Now when I hobble, it is an act
of mercy for that knee, the one
relied on so often in the sugar-beet fields.
I get somewhere; I relax, letting
me and the rest of the world balance
again. Take it easy, World, old friend.

William Stafford

THE GALL ANT

There are so many kinds of ant,
God can't name them *en passant.*
But of all the kinds there be,
The *Gall* Ant is the ant for me.
It is much nicer than the *Dorm,*
The *Blat,* the *Adam.* True to form,
It isn't like the *Tyr, Petul,*
Nor noisy as the *Baach, Ulul.* . .
Nor as the *Inf,* indeed, or *Ten.*
Not at all like the *Sycoph.* When
It speaks it does not give you lip
As the *Flamboy* and the *Flipp.*
Not calculating like the *Merch,*
Nor menacing as the *Comor.* Search

The whole ant kingdom, you will find
None nicer, unless *Pleas.* Its kind
Has close ties to the *Toler,* and
The *Conson* and the *Eleg.* Bland,
Still it, like *Trench,* can penetrate—
Not to be *Triumph.* A good skate,
Yet not as loose as *Err. Redund*
Is no relation, but *Abund*
Runs in its blood. No *Eleph;* though
Smaller, polished head to toe.

(Do not confuse Gall Ant with *gall;*
There's no relationship at all.)

John Fandel

THE DIGITAL WONDER WATCH
(An Advertisement)

When I look at the time,
it tells me the date,
the speed of my pulse,
my height, my weight.
It tells me how fast I'm
running, how straight.
It tells me my balance,
the dividend rate.
It tells me my birthday,
my license plate.
It's a wonderful watch!

Suppose I'm in London
and want to know

what time it is in Kokomo?
The weather in Miami or Maine?
How much sun or how much rain?
The name of the Daily Double to win?
Whether black or red
is the number to spin?
All I need do is look at the time.
It's elegant, neat, the size of a dime.
It's a wonderful watch!

It tells me my shoe
and my collar size.
It tells me the color of my eyes.
If I'm lost in the woods
it tells me North,
phases of moon and tide,
and so forth.
It tells me how hot I am, or how cold.
It tells me I'll never,
never grow old.
It's a wonderful watch!

Does it tell when the world ends?
And when did it start?
Does it show how to wind up a broken heart?
Well, that's in the works,
and of course, it's true
there's still to be added
a gadget or two,
to warn of earthquake, volcano, or war,
and how long the sun
will exist as a star.
Yes, it's a wonderful watch!

May Swenson

SELF-SERVICE

Always I wanted to do it myself
and envied the oily-handed boy
paid by the station to lift
the gun from its tall tin holster
and squeeze. That was power,
hi-octane or lo-, and now no-lead.

What feminism has done for some sisters
self-service has done for me.
The pulsing hose is mine, the numbers
race — the cents, the liquid tenths —
according to my pressure, mine!
I squeeze. This is power:

transparent horsepower, blood
of the sands, bane of the dollar,
soul-stuff; the nozzle might jump
from my grip, it appears to tremble
through its fumes. Myself,
I pinch off my share, and pay.

John Updike

MISS PIMBERTON OF

the Metropolitan
Museum of
Art
has the key
to
Genitalia.
The broken off

parts
of
Greek statues and
Roman gods
are her
curatorship.
From foreign countries

and graves,
papal quarters and
geological digs,
they find their way
to
Miss Pimberton,
who dates

the testicles, measures
penises,
labels all —
and files them
neatly,
deliberately,
working late.

Siv Cedering

2

SANGRIA & CHEESE

I am giving a party at which I am serving Sangria
And three of the ladies are crying.

I am serving Sangria & olives & cheese
To nine of my favorite fashionable ladies,

And three are sobbing and six are nibbling
And ten squeeze handkerchief hearts.

Ladies, my silk & trousered free-breasted ladies, please,
Enjoy your Sangria & cheese.

Bonnie Jacobson

A LINE FROM MARY MACLAINE

"I love my shoes!"
I, Mary MacLaine

I love mine too, Mary,
Yet but for you
Would I think to say so?

Your voice urged me
In the shower
And then again in bed, declaring:

Why not enter some room filled with people
And shout out for once the total truth?
"Delighted to see you! I love my shoes!"

Barry Spacks

FAMILY ECCENTRIC

Marie is bald and doesn't
give a damn. To prove it
she often spits in public
and hates to wear a hat.

I hope she changes
for the better before
she learns to talk.

Edward Willey

MISS CONEY ISLAND

The road to Nevada is paved with salt
from Utah, discarded California
sugar cones, and New York marriages
in Model A's that ran out of steam.

In Las Vegas I pawned my rat-fur coat
like a snake betting on spring.
I drank a shake and shook the hand
of a preacher whose eyes lit up like oranges.

And then I made love to the house dick,
who threw me over when he'd finished
dipping into my hip pocket. That's why
I couldn't make camel fare out.

Finally, I arrived on the coast
like Bertolt Brecht. Only the difference
was noticeable. They drank me down
like vintage Gallo wine for a season.

But now time turns to vinegar on my tongue.
I ask you, my life, not to run out on me
like all the others, my dreams, my waistline,
marriages, money, and those miserable slow horses.

You owe it to me after all I've given,
the hard years in transit, when sweat
rolled off my back like sequins
and I suffered without complaint.

John Morgan

A LADY

"Asshole" and "shit" were always on her lips;
   What other joys she sought mostly were oral.
     As she came puckering toward me, I advanced,
Then bent and kissed each of her fingertips,
   Well satisfied. It isn't that I'm moral
     Or elegant: I know she wipes her hands.

W. D. Snodgrass

CLERIHEWS

The Prince of Wales
Sent out for some snails.
He said, "It was on a State Visit to Fargo
That I developed a taste for escárgots."

Donald Hall

King of Lydia, Croesus
Had four wives and thirty-five "nieces."
His privy, I'm told,
Was lined with gold.

Ellen Glasgow
Thought human life a cruel fiasco.
And when Death murmured, "May I take your hat?"
Miss Glasgow bellowed, "How's that?"

Zane Grey
Struck pay
Dirt and
Quicksand.

Anne Boleyn
Did not care for woolen
Wear: she though brocade and crepe de Chine
Fitter for an English queen.

Paul Curry Steele

Leach, Alexander Archibald
has long been called
more elegant-
ly, Cary Grant.

Anonymous

When people said "Mister!"
To Owen Wister,
He replied (quick to rile):
"When you call me that, smile!"

Eva Marie Saint
Ain't
As famous as Liz,
But then who is?

Louis Phillips

MAISIE

"Fatty Arbuckle!"
she said.
I dieted.
She's dead.

Raymond Roseliep

FERKLE

Ferkle buys dirty books. They're just his speed.
Why though expend the money without need?
Fool, said his Muse to him, look in thy heart and read.

John Frederick Nims

POET'S EPITAPH

He always was an earthy gent;
Now he's in his element.

Michael McFee

FIVE POETS TALKING

She wants to hear the
                    meet
me
look, I had her without her
crack
        at 5:30

having me. And she had
Oh, her heart's in the right
                in the poet's voice
        MENS ROOM
        me?
        I never had her

                        place: now
if she could only find
                        the patience
        so we'd both had enough of
        her mind
                of a lizard
                catches flies
                        like a bull-whip

what we hadn't had
                in mid-air.

                                Peter Klappert

CHEZ T. S. ELIOT*

Too late to catch the last train home
    (a contretemps kind friends may spare us),
I sometimes spent the night at Tom's
    at 57 Chester Terrace.**

He and his first wife, Vivienne,
    were glad to put me up in, well, the
little front room of their small house
    between Belgravia and Chelsea.

When after one such night I woke,
    I saw the hall door softly open
—it wasn't even seven o'clock—
    and fingers, then a hand grope in

to full arm's reach and from its hook
    in the dim light, still as a ghost,
lightly lift off a bowler hat
    and disappear. It was my host,

of course, who with a burglar's tread
    and manner circumspect and nervous
was setting off, prayer-book in hand,
    to go to early Sunday service.

Robert Wallace

*After Herbert Read, whose account is quoted in
The Oxford Book of Literary Anecdotes, James Sutherland, ed., 1975.

**This Chester Terrace, in 1983,
is not the one in London A to Z;
that's way up north by Regent's Park somewhere.
Turns out, though no blue tile is mounted there —
the folks next door at 55 explain
(who took us in out of the cold May rain) —
the name changed more than thirty years ago:
so Chester Terrace is now Chester Row.
The Tube's Victoria, whence a short walk
a little west will let you stand and gawk.

RIDING HIGH

at the Museum of Coaches, Lisbon

When Clemente Eleventh went to tea
Or other Papal industry
He didn't take the train or bus
Like common ordinary us
But sat in most uncommon state
Resplendent in his coach and eight.
Indeed, it's down in Holy Writ
That Papa Clemente scored a hit
Each time he went among the masses
Preferring them to upper classes,
For living poorly in a hovel
Teaches one the art of grovel
And so they came from miles around
To be amazed and lick the ground.
They say the sight of the coach alone
Was blazing bright as God's own throne
Studded with jewels and covered with gilt
Conceived in heaven and custom-built.

On each right angle of the roof
Four cherubim played as if 'twere proof
That angels flew among the horses
Scaring off Satanic forces.
And six jeweled saints from the Holy See
Mingled with gods of mythology,
So all manner of belief
Protected the coach in bas-relief: —
St. Francis guarded locks and catches,
Aphrodite watched the latches —
Thus sex and sainthood strangely mingles
Causing chaste off-color tingles.
Athena too in Olympic splendor

Brandished her sword above a fender,
And even a lion or two made sure
His Holiness was kept secure
Or made to feel that by and large
Surrounded by that entourage
Papa Clemente would think it right
Indeed, quite proper in God's sight
If a beggar whose only thought was bread
Were struck by the coach and left for dead,
To trade in his life for a heavenly copy
Being bashed in the head by the Pope's jalopy.

Alice Friman

STEIN SONG

Saint Brigid wished Heaven an ocean of ale
And so I pray to become a whale.

John B. Harris

WORLDLY MONK'S SONG

O it's only a papal moon
    Floating over a cardinal sea,
And it wouldn't be "I believe"
    If you beleaguered me.

John Updike

YEARS LATER LITTLE JOHNNY
STOUT TELLS IT LIKE IT WAS

It was much worse
than Mother Goose told
in "Ding, Dong, Bell."
I climbed down the well
on slimy rope so old
it's a wonder Pussy and I
didn't end up drowned
in that silly verse.

It's never been said
but Tommy Lin
was sick in the head,
sickest kid in the county,
with a strange grin
and glazed eyes.

I was shovelling shit
in the barn when
Pussy's familiar cry
and the ringing of the bell
set the dogs barking

and me thinking,
"Who else but Tommy Lin."
I ran like hell!

He was hanging
half over the wall
spitting on the cat
as I came from behind.
For some reason I still
had the shovel in hand,
which I wiped clean
on Tommy's shirt
before I shoved him aside
and went down
for the deep meow.

The rest you know,
although I
might add that
once Pussy was in my arms,
shivering in my grip,
that little bitch
stuck one claw
clean through my lip.

Roger Pfingston

I GO OUT OF THE HOUSE FOR THE FIRST TIME

I go out of the house for the first time
since the day everybody found out
and the first person I meet says hello turd
so I pull off my ears I have always had

distinctive ears and drop them in a trash
dispenser in front of The Farmers Bank and a man
coming out of the bank says hello turd
so I twist off my nose as people have always
noticed my nose in particular and drop it in
the book deposit in front of the city library
and a woman coming out of the library says
hello turd and I begin to see
how difficult disguises are and pluck
my left eye out as people have always noticed
my eyes are most particularly well-matched
and swallow it down as there is no place to put it
and a small boy up a lamp pole says
hello turd so I pull off my penis
and everybody runs up saying in loud voices
look at the dumb turd he pulled off his penis

Miller Williams

THE TARANTULA

Everyone thinks I am poisonous. I am not.
Look up and read the authorities on me, especially
One Alexander Petrunkevitch, of Yale, now retired,
Who has said of me (and I quote):   my "bite is dangerous
Only
To insects and small mammals such as mice."
I would have you notice that "only"; that is important,
As you who are neither insect nor mouse can appreciate.
I have to live as you do,
And how would you like it if someone construed your relations
With the chicken, say, as proof of your propensities?
Furthermore,

Petrunkevitch has observed, and I can vouch for it,
That I am myopic, lonely and retiring. When I am born
I dig a burrow for me, and me alone,
And live in it all my life except when I come
Up for food and love (in my case the latter
Is not really satisfactory: I
"Wander about after dark in search of females,
And occasionally stray into houses," after which I
Die). How does that sound?
Furthermore,
I have to cope with the digger wasp of the genus
Pepsis; and despite my renown as a killer (nonsense, of course),
I can't. Petrunkevitch says so.
Read him. He's good on the subject. He's helped *me*.

Which brings me to my point here. You carry
This image about of me that is at once libelous
And discouraging, all because you, who should know better,
Find me ugly. So I am ugly. Does that mean that you
Should persecute me as you do? Read William Blake.
Read William Wordsworth.
Read Williams in general, I'd say. There was a book
By a William Tarantula once, a work of some consequence
In my world on the subject of beauty,
Beauty that's skin deep only, beauty that some
Charles (note the "Charles") of the Ritz can apply and take off
At will, beauty that—
                    but I digress.
What I am getting at
Is that you who are blessed (I have read) with understanding
Should understand me, little me. My name is William
Too.

Reed Whittemore

INDIGENOUS

"I am home," said the turtle, as it pulled in its head,
And its feet, and its tail. "I am home and in bed."

John Ciardi

HIPPOS

I'm very fond
of hippos *but*
I like them better
when they're shut.

Emily Otis

3

G-WHIZ

One thing about a gnat
I've gnever, gnever gnown
Is gnot the way it flies
Gnor that it's small full grown.

Gno, gneither is it that
When I would quickly bat
It in the gnose, the gneck,
Or back, the gnat is gnot.

Around a gnat I'm gnervous,
Unused to such a gneighbor
A gnet perhaps I gneed
To gnab it without labor.

By day as well as gnight
What gnags and gnudges me
Is gnaught but gnowing how
The gnat acquired that "g."

Richard Armour

LEARNING

Two-petalled, blue, with yellow stamens, this
Shy fellow halfway folded in his leaf
Grows almost furtively from the side of the stem
Whose top is occupied by two leaves opposite.

Small armies of him growing everywhere,
And yet his name not writ in any book
That I can find, so I have christened him
Nemerovia vulgaris, or Common Piss-Winkle.

Some people will do almost anything
To go down in history, get their names in the book.

Howard Nemerov

ON A NON-MIGRATORY FINCH

Insistent streak-spotting
In black on an off-white breast;
Seed-cracking bill; aggressive intolerance
Of other feathers that feed where you feed—
Purple finch, female, in winter rest
Far south of the finch nest
You emerged from, and other finches emerged from.

Heavy, half-southern spring grows late.
The male finches grew bright
Plumage, and left. The other females
Left. They are past the plains now, into the woods.
But you, ignoring the breeding flight,

Remain, always in sight
Of the seed-source you fed from all winter.

Are you, then, liberated?
Have you muttered in finchy spleen:
To hell with the pines of Ontario,
The nest to build, the clutch of streak-spotted eggs
Such a bore to brood, the keen
Labor of wresting from the green
World, food for all the insistent nestlings?

Forget it. I'll just watch
And keep seed running free
In the feeder usually closed for the summer
Weeks before now. I won't net you
In any verbal intricacy
Of the tiresome pathetic fallacy.
Whatever you are, you probably aren't pathetic.

W. R. Moses

THE WAY IT IS

Yell at the bad dog and the good dog cringes.
Yell at the good dog and the bad dog barks.

William Pitt Root

PASTORAL POEM

The shepherd husbands his sheep
The sheep may safely graze
All the way to the market

John Pauker

LINES ON THE UNTIMELY DEATH
OF A PET CANARY

O, the Durham heavens sobbed,
To have been so rudely robbed,
Of such a singer, in his prime,
At this the *melodye* time
For *smale foweles* like himself
Whose voice is their only pelf!

In Winter months his tongue would quake
But never the least music make,
Like a clapper in a tiny bell
Whose chime was muffled when it knelled.

Then Spring returned his song to him,
And well he loved his morning hymn,

Calling the abbess from her bed
To make sure he was showered and fed.

Here was a bird most celibate,
Who never madrigaled a mate,
But offered every heartfelt ditty
To God, Elaine, ungrateful Kitty.

That pampered cat perfidious
Snatched him from his breakfast lettuce,
Broke his song off in his throat
Before he raised another note.

Curse that feline so contrary!
Bless this innocent canary,
Who has flown our mortal coop
For a perch near Peter's stoop.
God of Being, guide Ken-Boid
As he migrates through the void.

Michael McFee

COUNTRY MATTERS

Summer nights a lit
candle is waxed fast
by Welsh farmers to
a tortoise's back,

then lowered by string
down to a slate cave
where a hare hides its
brown fur, wet eyes.

The mist off the field
is green as a leek;
he waddles in deep,
his wax wand erect

casting wobbling light,
his rear leg tethered
to the held breath of
night, bleak stars and air.

How like a wise man,
ponderous with care—
tortoise and candle
out hunting for hare.

Kenneth Rosen

SONG
TO COOKING OUT OVER AN OPEN FIRE
IN THE OPEN AIR
WITH CRICKETS GOING
Geechy   Geechy

Food gets brown and wood gets rose
And eyes join hands with ears and nose
To handle all of this that goes

    Fume rise

               juice drop

    Fpsss pif

               sssfpop

To thee oh Lord we lift the praise
For all this air in which to braise.

Roy Blount Jr.

SONG TO A NICE BAKED POTATA

If you find borscht
Down with bicarb must be worscht;
If *tripes a la mode de Caen*
Give you the creeps, overload and a paen;
If eating felafel
Makes you felafel—

Then: say to yourself, your spouse or waita,
"I'll have a nice baked potata."

It'll do you good, there is no question.
There's nothing it takes better to, than digestion.

It fits
You like pajamas do,
Your favorite pair.
It sits
On your stomach like you
On your favorite chair.

But on the other hand,
Just because it's bland,
Don't think that feeding yourself potata
Is just like feeding a processor data.

No, it's thoroughly
Existential.
Say your stomach's as blithe as Shoroughly
Temple and brazen as Walter Winchell.

Say it can handle hot dogs three
With onions and impunity.
And then, with both *sang-froid* and relish,

Chili that's so hot it's hellish;
Derma stuffed till it explodes,
And then four strudel a la modes—

The stomach of an alligata!

It will still appreciate a
Nice steamy baked potata.

(With sour cream, butter, bacon bits, chives.)
We have felt *fuller,* and so have our lives,
Whenever we ate a
Nice baked potata.

And you know it's a sin
Not to also eat the crumpled, crusty, butter-tinctured,
                                        vitamin-rich skin.
It looks like a shoe,
Or a bark canoe,
But there is no richer, more manifold chew.

Oh!
Idaho.

Roy Blount Jr.

& VICE VERSA

If you're inclined
to think that "Out of sight is out of mind,"
I recommend you ponder
"Absence makes the heart grow fonder."

Anonymous

AT EIGHTY MISS DICKERT BECOMES A PILGRIM

To see once more her sister Grace
Who lived outside of Providence,

She gave herself up
To the freeway.

Whatever the wide green signs overhead were saying,
They said so much and all at once

That her ancient black Olds
Slowed like a sea turtle miles from sea

And stopped.
Traffic passed her by like wind.

Richard A. Hawley

THE HUNT

I. Driving along the highway,
   I spot a shiny black lump on the road.
   Is it a wet rubber innertube
   Or a baby seal avoiding the hunt?

II. I stop along the highway,
   The shiny black lump on the road
   Is a wet rubber innertube.
   How did it get here from Alaska?

Terry O'Toole

THE WOLF AGAIN

Surely you remember, my darling, how Mrs Pig sent her three
little pigs out into the big world to make their fortunes—

For this story appears in your big red book and your little yellow
book—

And how the first little pig made his house of straw, and what
happened to him,

And how the second little pig made his house of sticks, and
what happened to him;

And you remember how the industrious third little pig refused to
make the mistake of his siblings, and built his house of
brick.

So that when the hungry capitalist wolf came huffing and
puffing to the sturdy brick house

He signally failed to do what he had done to the peasantry and
the lumpenproletariat,

But slowly and angrily worked himself up into climbing the roof
of the third pig's house to descend the chimney.

Of course we both know what the shrewd pig had been doing
in the meantime.

He had been boiling water.

Nowhere in Marx and Engels so far as I know, or even in the later writings of the anarcho-syndicalists, is there any suggestion that the revolutionary should boil water.

It has instead been the traditional assumption that at the crucial moment the revolutionary will step *out* of his house and attack the wolf.

Right here in this little story we find a unique insight into wolf psychology:

The wolf *had* to descend the chimney.

So the pig boiled water.

Now in the version of the story that you read in your big red book,

The wolf was cooked in the boiling water and eaten by the pig;

But in the version in your little yellow book he jumped out of the water, ran away and was never seen again.

When you are older you will discover that the author of the yellow book took the story from the red book but changed the ending so that you would sleep at night.

When you are older you will also learn of a curious modification produced by the CIA in which the wolf jumps out of the boiling water and eats the third little pig.

But I think you should know now that none of these stories is the true story.

In the true story the wolf, having been terribly burned by the
boiling water, leaps from the pot and has his burns cared
for by the third little pig;

And the pig and the wolf together then have an all-night
psychological "encounter" in which the wolf admits
to his evil ways and confesses to the pig that he had
planned not only to eat him but to use his skin for
capitalist wallets,

And the pig acknowledges that he had some sick-sick plans
too, such as going to bed with the wolf while the wolf
was convalescing;

And both as a result come to understand the important things
to understand,

Which are that the big bad wolf is not a big bad wolf but a
misunderstood wolf,

And the good industrious third pig is not a good industrious
pig but an anal and driven pig,

And both need therapy.

So they shake hands.

And apply for a joint grant.

Reed Whittemore

HAPPY HARRY

Happy Harry Hooligan,
Acting like a fool again,
  Kissed a frog
  That sat on a log
And jumped into the pool again.

Wesli Court

A NOSTY FRIGHT

The roldengod and the soneyhuckle,
the sack eyed blusan and the wistle theed
are all tangled with the oison pivy,
the fallen nine peedles and the wumbleteed.

A mipchunk caught in a wobceb tried
to hip and skide in a dandy sune
but a stobler put up a EEP KOFF sign.
Then the unfucky lellow met a phytoon

and was sept out to swea. He difted for drays
till a hassgropper flying happened to spot
the boolish feast all debraggled and wet,
covered with snears and tot.

Loonmight shone through the winey poods
where rushmooms grew among risted twoots.
Back blats flew betreen the twees
and orned howls hounded their soots.

A kumkpin stood with tooked creeth
on the sindow will of a house

where a icked wold itch lived all alone
except for her stoombrick, a mitten and a kouse.

"Here we part," said hassgropper.
"Pere we hart," said mipchunk, too.
They purried away on opposite haths,
both scared of some "Bat!" or "Scoo!"

October was ending on a nosty fright
with scroans and greeches and chanking clains,
with oblins and gelfs, coaths and urses,
skinning grulls and stoodblains.

Will it ever be morning, Nofember virst,
skue bly and the sappy hun, our friend?
With light breaves of wall by the fayside?
I sope ho, so that this oem can pend.

May Swenson

ROCKET BY, BABY

Rocket by, baby, in your space ship.
When you count down, the rocket will zip;
When you blast off, go into free fall,
And off will go baby, cockpit and all.

Wesli Court

ONE FOR CHILDREN

P's snobbish, head held haughtily.
R's nothing but a propped-up P.
A's first, and bears a point of pride.
B's like a camel on its side.
M: mountain peaks. V: going south.
S: curvy road. O: open mouth.
An F's an E that's lost its shoe.
A G pokes out its tongue at you.
I's feet are flat, and so's its hat.
U changed its mind. D's getting fat.
Y's branching out. Z zigs to zag.
X semaphores. Q shakes a leg.
But as for H, N, L, and K,
And W, and T and J,
I'm baffled as to what to say.

Barry Spacks

SOME DIFFERENCES

Dawn and Daybreak

Dawn is a thing that poets write
Verses about till late at night.
At *daybreak,* when the poets' eyes
Are closed in sleep, their neighbors rise
And put the coffee on to perk
And drink it, and go off to work.

Owl and Cat

An *owl* is like a *cat* because
Both pounce on rodents with their claws,
And look about the same in size,
And pierce the dark with round, bright eyes.
But cats are *beasts,* whereas an owl
Has wings, of course, and is a *fowl.*
An *owl* can fly up into trees
And then swoop down again with ease;
But when a *cat* is on a limb
A sudden dread can madden him
And make him howl, and grow still madder
Until some fireman brings a ladder.

Room and Moor

How is a *room* unlike a *moor?*
They're not the same, you may be sure.
A *room* has walls, a *moor* does not.
Inquire of any honest Scot
And he will say, I have no doubt,
That one's indoors and one is out.
A *room,* then, fits inside a dwelling;

A *moor* is its reverse in spelling,
And has such wild outdoorish weather,
Such rocks, such miles and miles of heather
All full of flocks of drumming grouse,
You wouldn't have one in the house.

Richard Wilbur

4

DALLIANCE TIME

The handsome, hearty, horny bear
Watches us watch and does not care.

The lofty lion keeps a date
With Lady Lioness to mate.

Sir Buffalo is clearly prime
To show his girl a gay old time.

How pleasant wandering through the zoo
At dalliance time, my dear, with you.

Bruce Bennett

SEX IN CONNECTICUT

In Hartford
They're too smartford.

In Bridgeport
They've no itchfort.

In Stamford
They don't give a damford.

In Milford
They send you a billford.

Westport
Is bestfort.

Pyke Johnson, Jr.

BOSS AND TYPIST

What she wants: being swathed in mink.
What he wants: her undressed, I think.
"So hopelessly opposed, those two,
There's just no way at all—" Says you.

John Frederick Nims

SIREN

I have known a number
of Elizabeths

each attracting me little
if at all
though the one that I met
at Rehoboth Beach
turned my continent thoughts
a bit naughtical

Robert Wheeler

USING HER HEAD, OR HOW TO
SALVAGE AN EVENING

As he was about to go, horny and glum,
she took it into her head to make him come.

Knute Skinner

THE LIGHTS OF LOVE

The ladies in my life, serially sexed,
Unscrew one lover and screw in the next.

J. V. Cunningham

HERBERT OF ROSELAND

(After "Sir Topaz")

A dark haired lady flits to Roseland dancing hall.
A trumpet spits a tango up the wall;
It twists around the red and purple drapes
To a domed ceiling the color of Italian grapes.

A saxophone hoots "Whaa, Whaa, Whaa";
Now dancers dance the Cha, Cha, Cha.
As slot machines are deaf to coins of lead,
Our lady's ears to suits of gentlemen seem dead.

Alone she sits on bench of grass green leather
With pots of paper roses in its top.
A vent above distributes spring-time weather.
She sips a glass of artificial lemon pop.

The dark haired lady wears a dress of raven cloth,
Around her neck, a nickel plated moth,
And in her hair its twin.
Why, dark lady, do you sit, while others spin?

Above you hang fixed stars of burnished chrome,
Those stars that guide all sailors home.
O stars that made Clytemnestra irate,
Led Othello to trust his mate too late,

Guard the lady who seems cold as sherbert,
For near the orchestral dais
A gentleman stares at her on the bias.
His name is Manuel Fernandez Herbert.

Manuel wears black pointed shoes.
He holds mainly rhythmical views.
His sideburns are fragrantly anointed;
His legs are loose and doubly jointed.

His only weapon is a switch blade knife.
A true Knight of Columbus,
A Master of the Art of Rhumbas,
At home he keeps six children and a wife.

The dark haired lady in a column mirror
Sees Manuel's sideburns glitter.
Her lemonade turns bitter.
She drops it in an urn marked "litter."

"Yes," her eyes do flutter,
Ascend Manuel as an elevator;
O hotter than steam iron on rumpled skirt,
Press up his shirt.

We leave them waltzing through imitation dark.
See them later at a subway in Central Park.
He fumbles on a stair for a turnstile token.
His plan: assignation over the waters in Hoboken.

Behind him, above upon the stair
The dark haired lady lifts a razor from her purse,
A wig from locks of genuine bleached blond hair.
Manuel turns, he sees, he starts a curse.

Too late! Mrs. Manuel Fernandez Herbert
Wipes a raspberry razor on his shirt,
Plucks the token from the hand
Now turning cold as sherbert.

Robert Watson

AT THE BAMBI MOTEL

Walls the color of old plums, a "tapestry"
above the bed: 4 dogs playing cards,
smoking cigars. One cheats, aces tucked
in his vest, squints at the schnauzer's
royal flush and sighs. A wall-size mirror
doubles the room, doubles the double
bed into something immense, a mattress
for a troupe of acrobats.
Where are we? How did we get here?
And most of all, where's Bambi?

I wouldn't, couldn't have dreamed
up this place if I'd read true romance
magazines for a year. In room 12,
someone's having a row with someone
else. *Cow!* he accuses her.
Pipsqueak! You call this a honeymoon!
she yells back. Fighting
must have a titillating effect.
Silence for a minute. The pop of a cork.
And then of all things, giggling!
I bet somebody's made the front page
of *The National Enquirer* staying here.
What if our room's broken into by mistake?
What if the guy next door is a senator,
the girl Miss Panty Hose of 1968?
I chain the door shut, tape the keyhole
under your doubting gaze.
Your eyes glaze over, you begin your
impersonation of a sex maniac
who can't get his clothes undone.
Sin makes us blush like innocents
nevertheless. . .
                                    I fall asleep
dreaming of Bambi. There's a forest fire!
I must get the dogs out! Intoxicated,
they dive out a window into a snowbank,
cards falling out of their clothes.
(Snow? An hour ago it was August!)
Room 12 lends the fire department champagne
to put out the flames. The senator's
distressed — Miss Panty Hose is more
undressed than I am. She grabs him
by the nose, makes him say "cheese"
for the photos. Where will we stay now?
The dogs are grateful. One knows

a place down the road, Roxie's.
"They treat you real good there," he growls,
"pink lightbulbs and wait till you see
what's on their walls. . ."

Elizabeth Spires

RUBAIYAT FOR SUE ELLA TUCKER

Sue Ella Tucker was barely in her teens.
She often minded her mother. She didn't know beans
About what boys can do. She laughed like air.
Already the word was crawling up her jeans.

Haskell Trahan took her for a ride
Upon his motorbike. The countryside
Was wet and beautiful and so were they.
He didn't think she'd let him but he tried.

They rode along the levee where they hid
To kiss a little while and then he slid
His hand inside her panties. Lord lord.
She didn't mean to let him but she did.

And then she thought that she would go to hell
For having let befall her what befell,
More for having thought it rather nice.
And she was sure that everyone could tell.

Sunday morning sitting in the pew
She prayed to know whatever she should do
If Haskell Trahan who she figured would
Should take her out again and ask her to.

For though she meant to do as she was told
His hands were warmer than the pew was cold
And she was mindful of him who construed
A new communion sweeter than the old.

Then sure enough, no matter she would try
To turn her head away and start to cry
He had four times before the week was out
All of her clothes and all his too awry.

By then she'd come to see how she had learned
As women will a lesson often earned:
Sweet leads to sweeter. As a matter of fact,
By then she was not overly concerned.

Then in the fullness of time it came to be
That she was full of child and Haskell he
Was not to be found. She took herself away
To Kansas City, Kansas. Fiddle-de-dee.

Fiddle-de-dee, she said. So this is what
My mother meant. So this is what I got
For all my love and whispers. Even now
He's lying on the levee, like as not.

She had the baby and then she went to the place
She heard he might be at. She had the grace
To whisper who she was before she blew
The satisfied expression from his face.

The baby's name was Trahan. He learned to tell
How sad his daddy's death was. She cast a spell
Telling how it happened. She left out
A large part of the story but told it well.

Miller Williams

THE COAST OF MAINE

Oh she was young and lovely and I was wise and free
We drove around the island, we camped beside the sea
I offered her my wisdom, she offered me her pain
But nothing ever came of it upon the coast of Maine

When we set out from Boston I guessed the time was right
The day was hot and sultry, summer was at its height
She talked of fear and frenzy, I spoke of violent ends
I knew we must be lovers and hoped we might be friends

Oh she was sad and lovely and I was fierce and free
We circled all the island and sat beside the sea
I murmured consolation as she poured out her pain
Yet nothing ever came of it upon the coast of Maine

She told me of her lovers as we sprawled on the sand
I gathered shells and pebbles and pressed them in her hand
We climbed a hill at sunset and gazed far out to sea
By God, I thought, she's lovely; thank God I'm young and free

The moon rose soft and silvery, night fell cool and clear
Tiny waves came lapping; I heard her breathing near
So I trundled out my wisdom; she countered with her pain
And nothing ever came of it upon the coast of Maine

We long have gone our separate ways but still I lie awake
And wonder what I might have done for love or pity's sake
If I had shown less wisdom, if she had brought less pain
We might have made a go of it upon the coast of Maine

Bruce Bennett

DEATH AND SEX

Tying my shoe
in sixth grade,
I tried not to look
up Leona Purdy's dress.

James Reed

A TEEN-AGER

The high-priced jeans, the new car—she got what
She wanted; she'd been taught to want a lot.
To her girl friend in back, she talked about
Which of her friends shacked up with which. I thought,
"That must be for my benefit. No doubt
She's younger than my daughter. Still, why not?
A glorious redhead. One helps ladies out."

Taking a cigarette, she had to switch
Hands on the wheel to pick a kitchen match
Out of her dungaree shirtpocket which
Seemed quite well filled. Then she reached down to scratch
Fire off those tiny steel teeth that meet, match
And catch closed where her trouserfly's dark patch
Curves under, brightly glittering in her crotch.

I'd seen truck drivers do that. The flames caught;
She lit and sucked in smoke. That's when I got
Snatched back down to facts; I knew why not.
She'd been so spoiled, groomed, fairy-story rich,
She thought hard talk and hard times could be bought
Like poor people's clothes to disguise your niche
In life. Why add my barrel to her notch?

W. D. Snodgrass

STEALTH

If I was going to break into your life
and steal what I could,
I'd take the bottom button from your oldest dress,
and three sticks of wood.

I'd steal a strand
of your hair from the bathroom sink, a bad
picture of you grinning, and the next-to-last
page of some old book you've never read.

Out of your cupboard I would swipe a glass
once filled with jelly; in your living room
I'd find a penny down inside the couch,
a crumb of candy fallen from your mouth.

I'd steal a dab of perfume from your Vanity;
all unused thumbtacks from your message board;
from your writing desk, one envelope,
and from your kitchen half an inch of cord.

I'd play your phonograph, and walk off with
your newest record's lyrics in my head,
and leave my handprints on your favorite chair,
my name inscribed upon your smoky air.

Ah love, you'd never miss a thing,
the needle from the rug, the tiny bedroom spring
I twisted off with pliers, nor see
how carefully I let you never steal from me.

Dick Allen

MY PENIS

Ordinarily I call it "my cock," but
often there is a strange formality about it,
this rocket with wattles.
"Penis" and "Vagina," a dignified couple

immobile on a Grecian urn
or at times engaged in elegant ballet and
desiring frequent medical checkups.
"Cock" and "Twat," two funloving kids
traveling from Pittsburgh to Tangiers
with a hundred bucks in their pockets,
laughing at Baptists but loving God.
Alone, it's
crazy and laughable, like the man
who stands up at every Quaker meeting,
testifying to his version of the Truth—
a drag to others but a private solace,
refusing to sit down when others whisper
"Shush," "shame," "time and place for everything" —
a dotty old turkey continually rising in wonder,
even on lonely winter evenings refusing
not to point to the stars.

Ed Ochester

TO A LOVER

The garlands and laurels
set on the foreheads
of those who fought best
sang best
on you
should be placed
lower
no
lower.

Lolette Kuby

FEAR OF CASTRATION

— A sharpened pencil is a shortened pencil.

In spite of everything my tender Mommy
Endured the member underneath my tummy
And while both rough and harsh she might have been
With cloth and nappy so to keep it clean,
She on occasion let it limply linger
Across an absent-minded, dainty finger
Or rubbed it some as if to give correction
To my misguided, premature erection.
But when she sat astraddle her own toilet
And something in my gonads cried "Uncoil it!
Unleash it skyward! Seige the battleax!"
I felt as well a batten on my sex
That makes all males when sticking out their necks
Uncertain whether, having put it in,
They'll get the bloody puncher back again.
Nobody knows (including me, I think)
How fearsome was that unrepentant sink!
To fall into that cavernous infraction
And suffer the unbearable subtraction
Would make the noblest peckermeister quail
When rising toward the pertly proferred tail.
How quick the sturdy whacker starts to droop!
As well take on the 13th Bomber Group
Or try the hive where bees are making honey
As penetrate one gaping, bearded cunny.
And if to lose your whanger isn't funny
Then how to contemplate the foul removal
Of that fair hanging fruit, at whose behooval
Senor Erectus masculates his charge?
Why, Caesar never would have Cleo's barge
Boarded, or Burton blunted bludgeon upon Liz

Unless the stroke of intermittent bliss
At one end of the shaft made them forget
The danger to what dangles at the other.
Was callousness like this what made my mother
Sit splayed as we have seen upon her toilet?
Ah, my poor seedlings, worthy of a soft
Caress and tender where they hung aloft,
Received instead a challenge that could drive
The staunchest bullock ne'er again to swive.
Poor darlings shrivelled, sought again the rings
Through which they'd dropt in search of better things
But as we know, they couldn't do that long
For tension in the testicles is song:
As quickly as the first note hits the strings
The baton rises, yearning to conduct.
As certain as our mothers have been fucked
That ancient music makes us take the plunge
And to its randy rhythm thrust and lunge,
For if we fear (and it's damn sure we do)
We'll lose our mammyjammer when we screw
That furry cavern, we'd rather take the chance
Than spend a lifetime creaming in our pants.

Dabney Stuart

TO A HUSBAND ON FATHER'S DAY

If you had been my dad I'm sure
I wouldn't be so insecure,
I wouldn't find the world so frightening,

I'd love injections, airplanes, lightning.
I'd be less tense and less impetuous,
But oh, my love, I'd be incestuous.

Linda Pastan

ORIGINAL SIN

The trouble with my ex-
   Was mostly sex.
The trouble with my new
   Is the to-do.
The trouble with them all
   Was Adam's fall.

J. V. Cunningham

AIRING LINEN

Wash and dry,
sort and fold:
you and I
are growing old.

Henry Taylor

5

POEM FOR MY WIFE

The hog-nosed snake, when playing dead,
lets his tongue loll out of his ugly head.
He lies on his back as stiff as a stick;
if you flip him over, he flips back quick.
If I seem dead when you awake,
please flip me once, like the hog-nosed snake.

Ted Kooser

ADAM AND EVE IN LATER LIFE

On getting out of bed the one says "Ouch!"
The other "What?" and when the one says "I said
'Ouch'." the other says "All right, you needn't shout."

Deucalion and Pyrrha, Darby and Joan, Philemon and Baucis,
Tracy and Hepburn—if this can happen to Hepburn
No one is safe—all rolled up into two,
Contented with the cottage and the cottage cheese
And envied only by ambitious gods. . .

Later, over coffee, they compare the backs of their hands
And conclude they are slowly being turned into lizards,
But nothing much surprises them these days.

Howard Nemerov

NATURAL HISTORY

The tickbird and rhinoceros
are not exactly friends;
still their long relationship
has served some common ends.

So love is not the only force
to hold two lives together;
if lowly ticks can harmonize
the hairy horn and feather

could there by such example be
another itch by which —
though you call me a bastard now,
and I call you a bitch —

some gentleness may seem a while
to make a kind of sense
and we might touch like lovers once
if not exactly friends.

Miller Williams

CORRECTION

Oh he loved her
Yes he did
With her sweet ass
And her tits tipped up
Like little hats
And her kiss-kiss-kisses
There was only one
Problem
Every time he said
"He don't. . ."
Her chicory-blue eyes
Fell
And she murmured
"He doesn't. . ."
Till finally one day
He didn't

Jane Flanders

BROWSERS

He flipped through the magazines
in the periodical room.
The Cadillac, he thought to himself,
is definitely the
Rolls-Royce of automobiles.

She sauntered through the stacks,
fingertips dusting
the tops of rows.
The things I don't know,
she shook her head sadly,
could fill a book.

They stand back to back
in the checkout line,
shifting their weights
from one foot to the next,

like two ships passing
in broad daylight.

Michael Finley

FABLE OF THE RETIRING CANDLE

A candle
Burned under
A bushel

He did not let his light shine forth
Among men

He did not even let his light shine forth
Among potatoes
The bushel was empty
(Being upside down)
And somewhat stuffy besides

They all called down to him
To come up on deck
And get some air
They wanted him to be the life of the party
To shine
Illuminate eternal verities
Set the world on fire
But no
He politely declined
He didn't want to come up on deck
And set the world on fire
All he wanted to do was stay down in the hold
And smoke
And curl up with a good book

Which he did

He smoked and curled up with
The poems of Yevtushenko
The Theory of the Leisure Class
Perrault the Duc de La Rochefoucauld
Erewhon and Through the Looking Glass
Also assorted Elizabethan sonnets

When he had finished
He put himself out
And went to sleep

Scott Bates

GARDEN GLOW

Plant a tulip bulb, and you
Will get a tulip from it.
The same is true of daffodils,
Sprung from a bulb to summit.

But here's what I would really like
Behind our humble cottage:
Old light bulbs I could plant and get
New bulbs of hundred wattage.

Richard Armour

FROM A POLISH CABARET

Man eats man; all just men know
    That's capitalism's curse.
Through sweat and tears, we've changed things so
    With us it's the reverse.

W. D. Snodgrass

TRAVEL TIPS

The trams in Amsterdam are yellow
    Or gray; in Oslo, blue.
In Copenhagen, bisexuals bicycle
    And take the buses too.
In Stockholm, by serene canals
    Big-bellied hotels float.
If you want to go to the Archipelago,
    You'd better take a boat.

John Updike

WHERE IS MY HALF-USED TUBE
OF TOM'S FENNEL TOOTHPASTE TONIGHT?

Here I am I think in Des Moines
in Dubuque, in Moscow Idaho
but where is my wandering luggage tonight?

Where is my little toothbrush?
Where is my bathrobe
slippery as wet rock
green as Saint Patrick's Day icing?

Are my black boots keeled over
under another bed?
Do my tampons streak across the night
little white rockets
trailing contrails of string?
Is some pervert fingering my bras?

Is a woman in Alaska dying for my red shoes?
Where is my purple dress in which my voice

is twice as loud, with the gold belt
glittering like the money I hope to get paid,
sympathetic magic to lure checks
out of comptrollers before time moulders.

I stink. My clothes stink. TWA stinks.
In this wastebasket of motel room
there's nothing of my own to rub
against my skin like a welcoming cat.

I feel like an imposter,
a female impersonator, a talking
laundry bag dialing head calls
to all my clothes in Port Huron,
in Biloxi, in Tucson, collect
calls into the night, I'm sorry
I spilled chili on you, chocolate
sauce, Elmer's Glue.
I'll wear an apron at all times.
I'll never again eat tacos.
O my wandering clothes, come home.

Marge Piercy

WE TARTARS

In Karakul hats and embroidered shirts
we Tartars are bodypersons, riding
our horses along the Steppes — we look
like Tartars, and we smell and taste
like Tartars: when we mate we mate
with Tartars through the Tartar night
from which come baby Tartars, bounced

on a knee, grabbing moustaches — such
is our way: we're Tartars, everyday.

If the good little God in His cleverness
had wanted trees instead of us,
or Englishmen, who could have stayed
His hand?

Barry Spacks

IN THE LAND OF RUMPS

> . . .leaving a place in the
> back of the mind for the ass. . .
>
> *Nostradamus*

What bespeaks the authenticity of the place
is the healthy behinds of the populace.
Beyond the merely picturesque, windmills and canals,
unreal as all tourist office images
(consider the dogshit on the sidewalks
everywhere and shameless) —
forget it, let it all pass:
There's nothing more authentic than
a big, beautiful Dutch ass.

The Capitol

Except for the medieval toytown center, the capitol
looks like it was built all at once in 1910 —
think of old Newark or Cleveland — dowdy then,
it achieves today an elegance, being perfectly preserved.
Here still reign windows of stained glass

above doorways of every economic class.
The streets' trim baroque-brick conformity
raises shudders inside at an old memory —
the Victoriana we painted over white,
doing everything we could to banish it from sight
in a revulsion that was generational
against mouldings, fireplaces, fixtures on the wall.
That it passed this city by seems like a miracle.
How the gloomy, the fussy, the gimcracky offended our eyes —
now it's hard even to remember why, though in part
I guess I'd blame the Museum of Modern Art.
But against the snug, smug style of these aging bricks
holding out against all turns of fashion,
our post-war passion to modernize
seems the more dated, and a trivial exercise.

The Economy

It's true they've got the biggest port in Europe
and one guesses that's more important than the tulip,
but with nothing but flowers, herrings, cows, and cheeses —
no raw materials at all — they're rich as Croesus.

The Land of Big Rumps

Chairs are built deeper, roomier, to accomodate it.
Pants, cut to the national shape, use more cloth
so there's more work for weavers.
In courting, face is unimportant
though round cheeks are ever popular,
and crucial to beauty contests is the heft
of the national treasure.
Knicknames are based on it:
High strutter, Perky, Droopy, Bunny Buns,
Flabby, Blabby, Wiggler, Poopy,

Bummer, Dumper, Got-the-Runs.
Of course a beer belly is a necessity
with its commitment to the local brew.
Otherwise, unbalanced, they'd fall over backwards.
But when bending down with rump in air,
say to tie a shoe,
it takes a lot of steam to get back up,
red-faced, puffing, hair askew.
The founder of the realm, Old King Rumper,
they say was worshipped from the rear
and homage paid with kiss posterior.
And though he rarely did, when he waged war
it was by personal combat with the enemy king —
King Rumper versus Bumper in the ring —
King Bumper had a reputation as a gooser.
They fought by bumping bums
in the royal rumpus rooms,
and afterwards the victor humped the loser.

The Queen

Just looking at her, you know
she has to be a healthy shitter,
shits well and anywhere, as indeed
she would have to, with her schedule —
she can't leave the state occasion to announce
I have to go to the bathroom, or do it in her pants.

She was obviously raised by a governess
who knew what life as queen was going to entail,
and in basics, raised her sensibly,
standing for no nonsense in that department —
the resulting sphincter control
would have to guide an empire after all.

Even high and mighty as she is
she has the look, like her neighboring island queen,
of someone who enjoys a good crap,
that is, when she gets the chance
to sit down on the can with the daily blatt,
even if alone is out and there has to be a lady-in-waiting
alert to sound of royal plopp and splatt,
ready to hand over swan's neck, terry towels,
toilet paper, and congratulations.

With their queen as example, the whole realm, surely,
on awakening moves its bowels,
beautifully, in concert, as a nation.

Edward Field

BRITISH WEATHER

It is the merry month of May,
when everything is cold and grey,
the rain is dripping from the trees
and life is like a long disease,

the storm clouds hover round like ghouls,
the birds all sing, because they're fools,
and beds of optimistic flowers
are beaten down by thunder showers,

under a weak and watery sun
nothing seems to be much fun—
exciting as a piece of string,
this is the marvellous British Spring!

Gavin Ewart

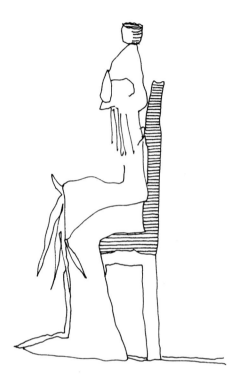

UPSTATE

"If Winter comes, can Spring be far behind?"
Where I live, yes: long months, so grim and glum
The snow lies blanker than a poet's mind
Who'd say a thing so pitiful and dumb.

Bruce Bennett

POOLWISE IN THE SAN FERNANDO VALLEY

We had this pad in Panorama City,
overnight a bedroom isle
where thousands of ranch-homes jostled
on what used to be one ranch.
From the air, you noticed aqua teardrops
weeping in every other back yard.
Gladly we shared our little Lake Canoga
with a parched family of Lockheed engineers
backed up to our fiberglas panels
which proved ingeniously removable.
We also waterwitched a mermaid from Reseda
who glittered cobalt from head to chin
in a scaley onto-staurus swimcap,
who dived and rose and all but Venused
in receding bikinis.
The land across the freeway remained less subdivided
its sharecroppers sticking to their shanty porch
except when 110 fahrenheit prompted them
to strip to their flannel drawers
and march across the speedlanes to our water
—punctuating the crazy progress of the cars—
father, son, grandfather, and great-grandfather.
The last turned out a distance swimmer and
of all our ornaments one of the most durable.

A. L. Lazarus

ON THE PROPOSED SEIZURE OF
TWELVE GRAVES IN A COLONIAL CEMETERY

Word rustles round the burying-ground,
Down path and pineconed byway:
The Commonwealth craves twelve heroes' graves
For a turn-lane in its highway.

Town meeting night, debate is slight —
Defenders of tradition
Twitter and cheep, too few to keep
The dead from fresh perdition.

His white-hot gaze emitting rays,
Selectman Ernest Earnwright:
'Some stupid corpse just wastes and warps
Where traffic needs to turn right!'

Embattled still within his hill,
One farmer loosed a snicker:
'When once ten redcoats dogged my arse,
I did not light out quicker

'Than when in a foss our scraps they'll toss
Therein to blend and nuzzle
Till God's last trump lift skull and rump,
One risen Chinese puzzle!

'Late yesterday as I listening lay
And the sweet rain kindly seeping,
I would have sworn I heard Gabe's horn —
'Twas but rush-hour's beeping.

'Ah, on my life! old Marth my wife
Will soon regret I chose her

When through our bosom-bones protrude
Posterity's bulldozer.'

Rose a voice in wrath from under the path:
'Why sulk we in this cavern?
Come, lads, to arms! — as once we formed
One morn at good Fitch Tavern!

'Are we mild milksops nowadays?
Do we not still resemble
The men we were, for all Time's wear?
Repair your bones! Assemble!'

But the first wraith gave a scornful laugh:
'With muskets long outmoded?
We'd stuff the crows like thrown-down grain
Before our barrels we'd loaded.

'For we dead,' mused Seth, 'but squander breath
On current ears. 'Tis plain
They'd amputate Christ's outstretched arms
To make a right-turn lane.'

X. J. Kennedy

6

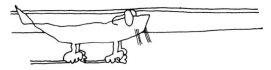

INVALID.KEYSTROKE

Wee.word.processor,.is.it.not
*De.trop.*of.you.to.put.a.dot
Between.the.words.your.nimble.screen
Displays.in.phosphorescent.green?

Your.cursor—tiny.blinking.sun—
Stands.ready.to.erase.or.run
At.my.COMMAND.to.EXECUTE
Or.CANCEL:.which? The.choice.is.moot,

So.flummoxed.are.my.circuits,.met
This.way.by.your.adroiter.set.
I.cannot.think..Your.wizardry
Has.by.some.ERROR.cancelled.me.

John Updike

REVISIONS

Great writers oft remind us
That we could make their works sublime;
For instance, if I had the time,
I'd rewrite some masterpieces,

Adding here, to fill in gaps,
Subtracting there the pages that annoy—
A little more of plot in Proust, perhaps,
And a little less of lecturing in Tolstoy.

Howard Moss

SPRING SONG FOR WILLIAM WORDSWORTH

My sod
leaps up:
a toad.

William Heyen

QUEER COUGHDROPS *

A readier supply of quail and Quaaludes
Would have cut down the glut of *Excursions* and *Preludes*.

William Harmon

*Homo Ludens

MADAM MARTHA GILBERT DICKINSON BIANCHI

How well I remember her, Emily's niece,
Who acted as though she were Emily's aunt,
Who looked like the Tragic Muse straight out of Greece
And cried out "I can" when the world cried "You can't."

Robert Francis

WITH APOLOGIES TO BASHO ET AL.

Haiku?

Fine, thanks.
And you?

★

Haiku!

Gesundheit.

Roger Pfingston

FRAGMENTARY RUMINATIONS ON THE CONTINUING PRESENCE IN THE WORLD OF JOYCE KILMER'S TREES

I think that I shall never see
A person rigid as a tree,
Although I have observed no other
Who stands so stiffly as my mother.

If a man scratch where it itches
He usually gets some on his britches,
Or finds beneath his underwear
A nest of blossoms in his hair.
Such a man, we know, is liable
To stern rebuke, *vide The Bible*.
Therefore, if God should make a tree
He'd be a fool, like you and me.

I think that I shall never see
Divine concern for forestry,
Doubting sincerely that God weeps
'cause Weyerhauser sows and reaps.

Poems lack mouths (hungry or sated)
And breasts (which may be overrated).
Anatomically, in fact,
They lack all features, front and back.
They neither clothe themselves, nor flow,
Aren't intimate with rain or snow;
Do not contend with cops or preachers,
Resist, quite passively, all teachers.
They have no hair, or nests for birds.
Poems lack everything but words.
How can they compete, I wonder,
With solid trees the earth stands under?
If for an instant I thought they should
I'd chop my pencil down, for good.

Dabney Stuart

THE ALCHEMIST

Who imitates
   Turns gold to quartz
And reading Yeats
   Writes Delmore Schwartz.

Donald Hall

PROGRESS

In the good old rhyming time
Dully Walter's verse would rhyme.
Rhyme!—it's out. So Walter won't.
Now his verses dully don't.

John Frederick Nims

HEAVENLY DAY FOR A DO: A PANTOUM

*(The Terrace. American Academy
and Institute of Arts and Letters.)*

"Heavenly day for a do!"
   "Here comes the Princeton contingent."
"They got Paul here — what a coup."
   "This punch tastes more like astringent."

"Here comes the Princeton contingent."
   "Mike Keeley and Joyce Carol Oates?"
"This punch tastes more like astringent."
   "That reporter's taking notes."

"Mike Keeley and Joyce Carol Oates?"
   "The proceedings were much too long."
"That reporter's taking *notes.*"
   "He looks just like Anna May Wong."

"The proceedings were much too long."
   "Look: there's Buckminster Fuller."
"He looks just like Anna May Wong."
   "A shame about Henry Miller."

"Look, there's Buckminster Fuller!"
  "Isn't there anything to eat?"
"A shame about Henry Miller."
  "His acceptance speech was *effete*."

"Isn't there anything to *eat?*"
  "Helen's wearing a schmata."
"His acceptance speech was *effete*."
  "Vassar's his alma mater."

"Helen's wearing a schmata."
  "Oh, Norman's dyeing his hair!"
"Vassar's his alma mater."
  "Watch out for that snake Alastair."

"Oh, Norman's dyeing his hair!"
  "They got Paul here — what a coup."
"Watch out for the snake Alastair."
  "Heavenly day for a do."

Robert Phillips

BONING UP FOR FINALS

End of term, will a six-pack do us
While we speed-read Upton Sinclair Lewis?
So far behind, can we possibly *ever*
Catch up on E. A. Robinson Jeffers?
Who said it was going to be multiple choice
On the later work of O. Henry James Joyce?
What's the plot of *The Rise of Silas Marner?* Who
Remembers the Swiss Family Robinson Cru-
Soe? Midnight late; one o'clock, tardy—
Was Laurence Sterne? Was Thomas Hardy?

Exposé: Was John Gay?
Oh God, let's have a break and all get mellow,
Take our chances on Henry Wordsworth Longfellow,
And maybe later give a lick and a promise
To the earlier lyrics of Bob Dylan Thomas.

Philip Appleman

A PLUMBER PRESENTS HIS BILL

"Shortened bathtub spout connection.
Caulked spout and spindle openings in tile wall."

It was poetry, she said.
But the style went bad after that:

"Labor and material. . . $13.14.
5% sales tax. . .   .66.

Total. . .   13.80."
It's impossible to make poetry out of money.

Louis Simpson

POETS OFTEN USE RHYME BECAUSE RHYMING MAKES CERTAIN IDEAS EASIER TO MEMORIZE

30 days hath April, June, & November,
& Harvey too hath 30 days
For driving without a license.

Louis Phillips

TO A POET ON THE EDITORIAL PAGE

Higgledy-piggledy
L. N. T. Nightingale,
Newspaper doggerel's
Your cup of tea—

Tepid, undrinkable,
Smothered in Sweet 'n Low,
Squeezed from a tired old bag
Penuriously.

Michael McFee

THE DEVIL'S ADVICE TO POETS

Molt that skin! lift that face!—you'll go far.
Grow like Proteus yet more bizarre.
  In perpetual throes
  Majors metamorphose,
Only minors remain who they are.

X. J. Kennedy

RHYME

Rhyme?—it's Apollo's zipper. Out of fashion,
What's to adjust the gaping fly of passion?

Jim Gregg

SORT OF A SESTINA:

In Partial Fulfillment of the Requirements

"What? You've never written a sestina?"
You gazed incredulous across your coffee.
"But I should think you'd take it as a challenge;
I mean, with all your fancy-work in form.
Well, if you ever write one, let me see it."
"I will," I promised. Here. I've kept my promise.

The thing is, I don't write things for the challenge.
Of course, when something's done I like to see it,
And once I start, it's sort of like a promise:
For instance, if I said, "We'll meet for coffee,"
We'd meet for coffee. It's like that with form,
And that's the way it is with this "sestina."

Don't get me wrong. I love to play with form,
And there's a certain pleasure in a challenge.
Again for instance, I've included "coffee,"
A word that doesn't have a lot of promise,
To say the least, for use in a sestina.
Once having used it, I'm obliged to see it

Through. Okay. Let's say I'm stuck with "coffee."
I need a spot to stick it, then I see it
And bang! (as right above) I've met that challenge.
That's what you've got to do with a sestina.
You pounce on any opening with promise
And score your piddling points against the form.

But having seized those openings with promise
And being well along in one's sestina
And every time it comes around to coffee

Sneaking another by to beat the form
's not such a grand achievement, as I see it.
Suppose you prove you're equal to the challenge—

The point is, what's the point? Who's going to see it
As anything but diddling with a form?
That's *why* I've never written a sestina.
It's always seemed a wholly senseless challenge.
But I remembered what you said at coffee;
And also, since a promise is a promise

(Even when it takes form as a sestina),
I'm hoping you may see it as a challenge
To promise we will meet again for coffee.

Bruce Bennett

THE VISITING GENIUS

A great bored toad
he quietly
observed
me
stuff my mouth
with feet.

Clemewell Young

ACUMEN

What critic can be more acute
 Than T. P. Random-Carper
Who pokes his pencils up his chute
 And bumps-and-grinds 'em sharper?

X. J. Kennedy

POET AND CRITICS

One hound that trots. A thousand fleas that ride.
Which way? A vote for each. The fleas decide?

John Frederick Nims

AT WRITERS' CONFERENCE

"Well, love me, love my dog." I'll cuddle the mutt.
"And love me, love my poetry." Love your *what?*
Look, I'm sweet Venus' champion. Not some nut.

John Frederick Nims

THE ORIGINS OF PSYCHOANALYSIS

"Money is shit," said Freud.
This utterance annoyed
Carl Jung, who much preferred
A less disgusting word.

Donald Hall

GNOTHI SEAUTON

The wise have known themselves. Some few
Recorded what it was they knew.
Then read those volumes on your shelves.
Who do you know who know your selves?

J. V. Cunningham

A CLASSIC SITUATION

What's pat in the Latin
And chic in the Greek
I always distinguish
More clearly in English.

Jane Flanders

AS THE CROW FLIES

Ten miles as the crow flies
we've often said, although
we cannot really say for sure
just how the flight will go.
What happens if he meets en route
a lovely lady crow?

Darrell H. Bartee

FEAR ITSELF

FDR said it foremost
having used as his ghost

writer Emerson, Emerson
(also Thoreau & the Duke of Wellington)

having brought home his Bacon, Bacon
having reaped Montaigne, Montaigne

having absorbed Publilius Cyrus, Publilius
when timorous

(of death in particular)
having plucked it from the vernacular

for, as immortal Seneca has said
(with all the generous dead)

The best ideas are common property.
He also said, What fools these mortals be.

Copyright nineteen eighty one,
Bonnie Jacobson

THE RIME OF THE ANCIENT MAGAZINE

For *The Atlantic's* 125th birthday
October 19, 1982

Eleven editors have proudly heard
   The Western Ocean roll
Since Boston's Best were briskly stirred
   By Jamie Russell Lowell.

Come war, come peace, the issues moved.
   What harvests! Rising yields
For Concord lettermen, approved
   By handsome James T. Fields!

Then days of fire and frost obtain.
   Chill seizes Boston's bowels,
Though on the bridge with James and Twain
   Stands stalwart William Howells,

Who yields, alas, to Gotham's gold,
    Aspiring to be called rich,
And Park Street takes into its fold
    Young Peck's bad boy, Tom Aldrich,

Whose style, erratic, overdressed,
    ("See, Ma! No hands! No rudder!")
Is soon corrected and compressed
    By H. Elisha Scudder.

He, overworked, was soon retired.
    The century slipped its cage,
But not before someone had hired
    A man named Walter Page

Who came, who went. A dreadful mess.
    The Mifflins were not merry
and turned, with limited success,
    To bland and blissful Perry.

And then — they sold the Magazine.
    (Not many men had sought it.)
In his calm confidence serene
    Young Ellery Sedgwick bought it

And steered the ship for thirty years,
    Repairing all her leaks
Until not many months before
    He piped aboard Ted Weeks

Who took his trick for twenty-eight,
    The fires of culture fanning
Our first centennial. The hand of fate
    Then seized on Robert Manning

To spur and sit this balky steed.
  Dame Fortune thought his sit worth
A scion worthy of the breed
  Like gentle William Whitworth.

My story's told. The Atlantic's sold
  From sea to shining sea,
from Eighteen Fifty-Seven's A
  To this year's modest Z.

Peter Davison

7

POLLUTED MOTHER GOOSE

Mary Mary quite contrary
How does your garden grow?
With Ford sedans and Miller cans
And coke bottles all in a row

   Hush-a-bye birdy
   On the tree top
   When the wind blows
   Your breathing will stop
   When the wind dies
   Your feathers will fall
   And down will come birdy
   Springtime and all

Jack and Jill went up the hill
To fetch a pail of water
Jack came down with hepatitis
And Jill came down soon after

Scott Bates

A RED SKIRT

A flea bit my man to death
way up in the forest.
My eyes cried, my heart smiled.
Sorrow ran in the forest.
God be praised, my man is dead.
Now I can eat my food without bread,
wash dishes once a month or not,
go to bed with dirty feet
and dance with a red skirt on.

Siv Cedering

SHE HAD HOPED FOR A SIGN

Two days the fart
had grown inside him,
then it came,

sweet and vulgar,
like a machine-gun
sunk in honey.

His widow smiled
thinly.

Michael Finley

A VEGETABLE LIFE

The artichoke
is the tortoise of vegetables.

It writes home:
"Dear Parents,
            Yesterday we had a contest.
            Out of the whole class,
            I came in thirty-fourth.
            Hooray!"

Eve Merriam

HAIKU

Nice Guy is a man
Who does what he ought to do
Without abandon.

Richard Wilbur

PRACTICE

Practice is a form of failure
Famed for giving heart
To those who'll never finish though
They start, and start. And start.

William Pitt Root

DEAR B—

You have invited me out
for croquet, for badminton,
for a walk around the lawn.
You have invited me to come
on Friday for a weekend
in the sunlight that drains
from your sky.

I regret. . .
my sinuses. . .my hemorrhoids. . .
I pulled. . .I fell over. . .

You would do well
to consider me ungrateful.

Peter Klappert

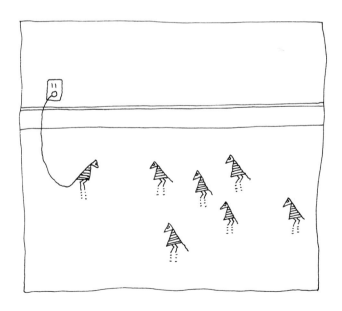

TEXT FOR A FORTUNE COOKIE

Life is dirty, rotten game.
You know some others?

Richard Moore

WHAT HAPPENS

What happens if I deduct six from ten?
I get four, but what happens to four?
It stands alone, on the outside
looking in, with nothing to do
but stand there by itself,
bored, unhappy, restless and waiting
to do something besides being itself.

After all, to be itself only—
what does that mean? No more
than if I were to say a tree is a tree.
Does that make you want to touch one?
No, therefore something must be done
about four left over from ten.
We must rally around it
and bring it into our booming
economy and culture.

David Ignatow

I LEARN I'M 96% WATER

and stare out over the edge of this little
dinghy I've named The 4 Percent. Such
a large sea. . .! Such a tiny
motor: this spermtail whipping like crazy. . .!
"The sailor *is* the sea." How
Zen! I float in my floating.
The body bobs in its life.

Albert Goldbarth

THE BALLAD OF JIM HIATT

Jim Hiatt was sort of a quiet man
Who lived at the edge of our town
In an old Chevrolet insulated with hay
And geraniums growing around.

As a boy he was shy, the old folks would sigh,
And his ma did the talkin' for him:
"Jim's tickled pink by that nickel, sir;
That's right, now, ain't it, Jim?"

Her name was Marie, of the dimpled knee,
Of the curls and the glittering eye,
And she wore such short skirts that sometimes it hurt
To see her go scampering by.

She lit out each night for the neon lights
Where she served polish sausage and beer,
While Jim's pa, with a stare, sat there dumb in his chair,
An unemployed auctioneer.

Jimmy's nights were each spent by the Atwater-Kent,
Entranced by the voices he heard,
And he loved Edgar Bergen and how he could work in
A funny from Mortimer Snerd.

His ma was contrite when she'd stayed out all night:
"Jim, honey, it's money, not fun.
For as long as I'm able, I'll keep waitin' table
To buy you a dummy, too, son."

Then she'd give him a dime, ten cents at a time,
Which he put in an old pickle crock,
And he saved all his money to buy him a funny
Wood dummy that he could make talk.

Jim's daddy took off with a whore from Decorah
One winter and never came back;
He'd been fixin' to live off the tricks of that vixen,
But they found him in halves by the track.

At the end of ten years of bills in arrears,
Jim had saved up enough for a dummy,
And it came C.O.D., carved out of a tree,
With levers and wires in its tummy.

So they went off together, young Jim and his mother,
To travel the world with a show,
But she found the first day, to her speechless dismay,
Jim had no voice to throw.

Marie was plain horrified, she'd hoped to be glorified
On a limelighted stage with her Jim,
Till she saw through her tears he'd been mute all these years;
Not one syllable came out of him.

So they came home again, on the very same train
That had cut Jimmy's daddy in two.
Marie's heart was broken that Jim hadn't spoken,
And even the dummy looked blue.

She got back her job as a waitress at Bob's,
But the fire had gone out of her eyes,
And she lost all direction, got a social infection,
To nobody's special surprise.

She died in her bed, with delirious head.
Jim was watching a show on T.V.
And when she reached land, she was holding the hand
Not of Jim, but the dummy, you see.

Ted Kooser

YOU CAN'T QUIT, YOU'RE FIRED

Just as the man stepped
off the chair and into
the noose the building
shook, the walls caved in
and a wall of water
18 feet at the crest
swept into the room.

Michael Finley

FAT LENA'S RECIPE FOR CROCODILE SOUP

First, run around in circles
until you drop.
The crocodiles will come
and eat you up.
Then your grandmother
must enter the room
with her ax and chop
the heads off the crocodiles.
She will know how to add water,
salt, pepper, onions and butter
to make a delicious
soup out of them.

Phyllis Janowitz

TURN ABOUT IS FAIR PLAY

The undertaker undertakes
An undertaking some call plunder.
He, so it seems, has all the breaks
Until he too is taken under.

Robert Francis

THE COKE MACHINE

The Coke machine that robs you will pay up,
will give you two cups, one day, in your cup.

Harold Tinkle

ENERGY: A VILLANELLE

The log gives back, in burning, solar fire
   green leaves imbibed and processed one by one;
nothing is lost but, still, the cost grows higher.

The ocean's tons of tide, to turn, require
   no more than time and moon; it's cosmic fun.
The log gives back, in burning, solar fire.

All microörganisms must expire
   and quite a few became petroleum;
nothing is lost but, still, the cost grows higher.

The oil rigs in Bahrain imply a buyer
   who counts no cost, when all is said and done.
The logs give back, in burning, solar fire

but Good Gulf gives it faster; every tire
   is by the fiery heavens lightly spun.
Nothing is lost but, still, the cost grows higher.

So guzzle gas, the sunless night draws nigher
   when Man's sheer soul shall keep him on the run.
The logs give back, in burning, solar fire;
nothing is lost but, still, the cost grows higher.

John Updike

RESPONDING

Hearing the furnace he thought
of a floppy forgetful fat woman

bestirring herself to her chores
pushing herself through
her guilt-ridden labors so fast
she is forced to collapse
with a loud swish and woompf
into silence at last

Then he thought he heard her
start up again
the song of the flame
for a little one bright in the face

He listened and it laughed
at her round red eye
her big black mouth

He watched and she rubbed
its little white head
and seeing she stopped
and winked such an eye
with being so pleased

he caught himself wishing
never to start her up again
but he liked it so much
he did anyway

Edwin Honig

THE ISLE OF CAPRI

Twas on the Isle of Capri that I met her
rowing a glass bottom boat

along with a Roman professor
who said the name of the island meant "goat."

She rowed us into a grotto
where the bubbles were bursting like fire
I didn't know whether I ought to
but decided I might as well try her.

Capriciously I addressed her
there on the Isle of Capri
but she said she loved the professor
him and his little goatee,

and I was the one he was after
the professor said sheepishly;
that was the end of our caper
on the classical Isle of Capri.

Dick Barnes

DOUBLE DACTYLS

Higgledy-piggledy
Hopalong Cassidy
Played in the movies by
Actor Bill Boyd

Why he was saddled with
Orthopedistical
Problem's a matter for
Doctor S. Freud.

Higgledy-piggledy
Thomas A. Edison
Dreamed up the phono as
Well as the light

Thanks to his genius e-
Lectromechanical
We can read labels of
Records at night.

Higgledy-piggledy
Euclid Geometer
Pained by the asking of
"What is the use

Studying doctrines so
Axiomatical?"
Answered acutely, "Oh,
Don't be obtuse!"

Higgledy-piggledy
Hyman G. Rickover
Fathered our Navy's great
Nuclear might

Thanks to the work of this
Annapolitico
Much of our arsenal's
Deep out of sight.

Anthony Harrington

MORE

I have heard them all yes heard them all already
Yet go daily
For more and more of a moreness that is like a
Jackal etherized upon a tape deck
While from under the stage comes the voice of a ghost that saith
Swear kid
To listen not no more not nevermore
To all that more
   It's lead in your bad ear dear
   Hear?
Have heard them all yes heard them all and sit
Way way down in my bone house boning up
On whether 'tis nobler in mind to suffer the more more
Or pull the switch
On Rather, Reynolds, Mudd and Jessica Savitch
Forevermore.

Reed Whittemore

FOR AN ELDERLY ACADEMIC

Because ripeness is all
and he wants to please
he decays tastefully,
like expensive cheese.

Ed Ochester

MATH PROBLEM POSING AS POEM

He stroked his beard,
and wondered how long
it would take to travel one hundred miles
if you started at one hundred miles per hour
and slowed down one mile per hour for each mile travelled.

Terry O'Toole

CHALIB DECIDES TO BE RETICENT

There is a question I would like to ask
the world. But I don't think I will ever ask it.

Strange to think — I have thought too far
and now must hide a discovery.

I couldn't make the world, or even change it,
but I can find something here and keep it before I go.

Friends, if you knew what I'm talking about
you would be glad that I didn't tell you.

William Stafford

POETICS

You know the old story Ann Landers tells
About the housewife in her basement doing the wash?
She's wearing her nightie, and she thinks, "Well hell,
I might's well put this in as well," and then
Being dripped on by a leaky pipe puts on
Her son's football helmet; whereupon
The meter reader happens to walk through
And "Lady," he gravely says, "I sure hope your team wins."

A story many times told in many ways,
The set of random accidents redeemed
By one more accident, as though chaos
Were the order that was before creation came.
That is the way things happen in the world:
A joke, a disappointment satisfied,
As we walk through doing our daily round,
Reading the meter, making things add up.

Howard Nemerov

ACKNOWLEDGMENTS

All poems not listed hereunder are printed here for the first time; copyright remains vested in the poets. The following poems, previously copyrighted, are reprinted by permission of their authors or as otherwise indicated.

Richard Armour. "G-Whiz" first appeared in The Saturday Evening Post and "Garden Glow" in The Wall Street Journal; both © by Richard Armour.

Scott Bates. "Fable of the Retiring Candle": © 1969 by Scott Bates; reprinted from The New Republic. "Polluted Mother Goose": © 1982 by Highlander Research and Education Center; reprinted from The ABC of Radical Ecology by Scott Bates.

Bruce Bennett. "Sort of a Sestina": © 1980 by Bruce Bennett; first appeared in Pequod.

Siv Cedering. "Miss Pimberton of": © 1975 by Siv Cedering; reprinted from Mother Is (Stein and Day). "A Red Skirt": © 1980 by Calliopea Press as a Color Poems Post Card.

J. V. Cunningham. "The Lights of Love," "Original Sin," and *"Gnothi Seauton":* © 1980 by J. V. Cunningham; first appeared in The New Republic.

Michael Finley. "She Had Hoped for a Sign": © 1975 by Michael Finley; first appeared in Great Circumpolar Bear Cult; reprinted from Lucky You (Litmus Press).

Jane Flanders. "Correction": © 1978 by Jane Flanders; first appeared in The New York Quarterly. "A Classic Situation": © 1960 by Jane Flanders; first appeared in Bryn Mawr Alumnae Bulletin.

Albert Goldbarth. "I Learn I'm 96% Water": © 1976 by Albert Goldbarth; first appeared in Bits.

Anthony Harrington. "Double Dactyls": © 1982 by Anthony Harrington; reprinted from Tersery Versery (Hendricks Publishing, P.O. Box 724026, Atlanta, Georgia 30339) by permission of Ron Hendricks.

Richard A. Hawley. "At Eighty Miss Dickert Becomes a Pilgrim": © 1982 by R. A. Hawley; reprinted from With Love to My Survivors, Cleveland State University Poetry Center, No. 31.

William Heyen. "Spring Song for William Wordsworth": © 1980 by William Heyen; first appeared in Bits.

Bonnie Jacobson. "Sangria & Cheese": © 1981 by Bonnie Jacobson; first appeared in On Being Served Apples (Bits Press). "Fear Itself": © 1981 by Bonnie Jacobson; first appeared in The Gamut.

Phyllis Janowitz. "Fat Lena's Recipe for Crocodile Soup": © 1974 by Phyllis Janowitz; first appeared in Arion's Dolphin.

X. J. Kennedy. "On the Proposed Seizure of Twelve Graves in a Colonial Cemetery": © 1982 by X. J. Kennedy; first appeared in Ploughshares. "The Devil's Advice to Poets": © 1981 by X. J. Kennedy; first appeared in Times Literary Supplement in England, in Wittenberg Review in the U.S. "Acumen": © 1981 by X. J. Kennedy; first appeared in The Massachusetts Review.

Peter Klappert. "Five Poets Talking": © 1973 by Peter Klappert; first appeared in *beyond baroque.* "Dear B—": © 1981 by Peter Klappert; first appeared in *waves.*

A. L. Lazarus. "Poolwise in the San Fernando Valley": © 1970 by A. L. Lazarus; reprinted from Entertainments & Valedictions (Windfall Press).

Eve Merriam. "A Vegetable Life": © 1976 by Eve Merriam; first appeared in Bits.

John Morgan. "Miss Coney Island": © 1972 by John Morgan; first appeared in Chelsea.

Howard Nemerov. "What Kind of Guy Was He?": © 1973 by Howard Nemerov; reprinted from Collected Poems (University of Chicago Press). "Learning," "Adam and Eve in Later Life," and "Poetics": © 1982 by Howard Nemerov; first appeared in Poetry.

Ed Ochester. "Monroeville, Pa.": © 1981 by Thunder City Press; reprinted from A Drift of Swine by permission of Thunder City Press; first appeared in The Midatlantic Review. "My Penis": Reprinted from Dancing on the Edges of Knives by Ed Ochester, by permission of the author and the University of Missouri Press: © 1973 by Ed Ochester.

Louis Phillips. "When people said 'Mister!'" and "Eva Marie Saint": © 1980 by Louis Phillips; reprinted from Quick Flicks.

James Reed. "Death and Sex": © 1978 by James Reed; reprinted from Morning Notes to a Nighttime Diary (Bits Press).

Knute Skinner. "Using Her Head, Or How to Salvage an Evening": © by Knute Skinner; first appeared in Poetry Now.

W. D. Snodgrass. "A Lady" and "A Teen-Ager": © 1981 by W. D. Snodgrass; first appeared in Tygers of Wrath, X. J. Kennedy, ed. (The University of Georgia Press).

Elizabeth Spires. "At the Bambi Motel": © 1979 by Elizabeth Spires; first appeared in Poetry; reprinted from Boardwalk (Bits Press).

Paul Curry Steele. "Clerihew" (Zane Grey): © 1976 by Paul Curry Steele; reprinted from Anse on Island Creek by permission of Mountain State Press; first appeared in Bits.

Harold Tinkle. "The Coke Machine": © 1976 by Harold Tinkle; first appeared in Bits.

John Updike. "Self-Service": © 1979 by John Updike; first appeared in The Atlantic. "Travel Tips" and "Worldly Monk's Song": © 1978 and 1980 by John Updike; first appeared in Bits. "Energy: A Villanelle": © 1979 by John Updike; first appeared in The New Yorker. "Self-Service" and "Energy: A Villanelle" are reprinted from Five Poems (Bits Press, 1980).

Reed Whittemore. "The Tarantula": © 1959 by Reed Whittemore; reprinted from The Self-Made Man (Macmillan). "The Wolf Again": © 1974 by Reed Whittemore; reprinted from The Mother's Breast and the Father's House (Houghton Mifflin) by permission of the author.

Richard Wilbur. "Some Differences": © 1981 by Richard Wilbur; first appeared in The Massachusetts Review.

Miller Williams. "I Go Out of the House for the First Time": © 1973 by Miller Williams; reprinted from Halfway from Hoxie (E. P. Dutton). "Rubaiyat for Sue Ella Tucker": © 1981 by Miller Williams; first appeared in New England Review. "Natural History": © 1981 by Miller Williams; first appeared in The Chariton Review.

INDEX OF POETS